ROSEN ✓ Verif

CURRENT ISSUES

T0023239

IMMIGRANTS
AND
REFUGEES

Carol Hand

ROSEN
PUBLISHING

New York

Published in 2021 by The Rosen Publishing Group, Inc.
29 East 21st Street, New York, NY 10010

First Edition

Editor: Amanda Vink
Book Design: Reann Nye

Photo Credits: Cover Nicolas Economou/Shutterstock.com; Series Art PinkPueblo/Shutterstock.com; p. 5 Vic Hinterlang/Shutterstock.com; p. 7 Ververidis Vasilis/Shutterstock.com; p. 9 George Frey/ Getty Images News/Getty Images; p. 10 Print Collector/ Hulton Archive/Getty Images; p. 11 ilbusca/iStock/ Getty Images Plus/Getty Images; p. 13 George Rinhart/ Corbis Historical/Getty Images; pp. 15, 24 Everett Historical/Shutterstock.com; p. 17 (top) ullstein bild Dtl./ ullstein bild/Getty Images; p. 17 (bottom) https://commons.wikimedia.org/wiki/File:Mabel-lee-chinese-student-monthly-1915-sm.jpg; p. 19 Wally McNamee/ Corbis Historical/Getty Images; p. 21 Rebekah Zemansky/Shutterstock.com; p. 23 Chintung Lee/Shutterstock.com; p. 25 (top) PhotoQuest/Getty Images; p. 25 (bottom) MICHAEL TRAN/AFP/Getty Images; p. 26 VIEW press/ Corbis News/Getty Images; p. 27 The Washington Post/Getty Images; p. 29 John Moore/Getty Images News/Getty Images; p. 31 John Moore/Getty Images News/Getty Images; p. 33 Erik McGregor/LightRocket/Getty Images; pp. 34–35 MARIO VAZQUEZ/AFP/Getty Images; p. 37 Handout/Getty Images News/Getty Images; p. 39 David A. Litman/Shutterstock.com; p. 41 Justin Sullivan/Getty Images News/Getty Images; p. 43 ANDREAS SOLARO/AFP/Getty Images; p. 45 Sanchai Kumar/Shutterstock.com.

Cataloging-in-Publication Data

Names: Hand, Carol.
Title: Immigrants and refugees / Carol Hand.
Description: New York : Rosen Publishing, 2021. | Series: Rosen verified: current issues | Includes glossary and index.
Identifiers: ISBN 9781499468465 (pbk.) | ISBN 9781499468472 (library bound)
Subjects: LCSH: Immigrants–United States–Juvenile literature. | Refugees–United States–Juvenile literature. | United States–Emigration and immigration–Juvenile literature.
Classification: LCC JV6465.H33 2021 | DDC 304.8'73–dc23

CPSIA Compliance Information: Batch #BSR20. For Further Information contact Rosen Publishing, New York, New York at 1-800-237-9932.

Find us on

CONTENTS

LEAVING HOME

Humans have always moved from place to place. Sometimes, they move away from their country of birth. They cross a border into a new country. These people are called migrants.

A migrant is anyone who moves to another country. Migrants may later return home or stay in the new country. They may become citizens of the new country. Or they may not.

People migrate, or move, for many reasons. But they all want a better life. They may want to find work, get an education, or be with family. They may want to be safe from dangers in their home country. They may have to move because of a natural disaster.

Migrants from Honduras board a truck to travel to the United States.

WHY PEOPLE IMMIGRATE

Some people enter the United States from another country and choose to stay. This type of migrant is called an immigrant. Immigrants must follow rules to stay in the country. Some of them become citizens.

People in the United States can ask the government to allow a **relative** to immigrate, or to come live somewhere in the country.

KINDS OF MIGRANTS

- **Immigrant:** A person who travels to another country to live there.

- **Refugee:** A person who leaves their own country to avoid danger.

- **Asylum seeker:** A person who has left their own country but has not yet been accepted as a refugee.

Many of the world's refugees are children.

✔ VERIFIED

The U.S. Committee for Refugees and Immigrants helps people who have left their home country. They **protect** immigrants' rights and meet their needs. Learn more here: **https://refugees.org/**

THE FOUR IMMIGRATION CLASSES

People in the United States fit into one of four immigration groups.

Citizens are either born in the country or are **naturalized**. Naturalized citizens have lived in the country for several years and met the requirements to become citizens.

- **Legal permanent residents (LPRs)** have a "green card." This gives them **permission** to live and work in the United States.

- **Nonresidents** are allowed to be in the country but can't stay. They include students, tourists, and people engaged to be married.

- **Undocumented** people are here without permission.

- **U.S. Citizens** are people who were either born into the United States or who have become naturalized.

People take an oath, or make a promise, when they become naturalized citizens.

EARLY U.S. IMMIGRANTS

The **colonial** period of American history began the story of American immigration. French and Spanish settlers began arriving in the 1500s. The first permanent English settlement began in 1607. It was at Jamestown, in what is now Virginia.

A small group, including many people seeking **religious** freedom, settled in what is now Plymouth, Massachusetts. These were the Pilgrims.

The Pilgrims landed at Plymouth Rock in 1620.

INDENTURED SERVANTS

Many people couldn't pay to immigrate. They became indentured servants. They signed a contract agreeing to work for a certain number of years. They were brought to the colonies and given food, clothing, and a place to live.

THE ENSLAVED

Enslaved people were forced to come to the New World. They arrived from West Africa in 1619. Between the 1600s and 1800s, up to 650,000 Africans were brought to America and sold into slavery.

LATER U.S. IMMIGRANTS

Between 1815 and 1865, new waves of immigrants came to America from Europe. Most were very poor. They wanted better jobs and better lives.

Ireland suffered a great **famine** in the mid-1800s. About one-third of U.S. immigrants during this time came from Ireland. Most settled in cities on the East Coast.

Beginning in the 1850s, many Chinese immigrants came to the United States. Some came for the California gold rush. Others built railroads, worked in clothing factories, and did farmwork.

Industries and cities both grew quickly between 1880 and 1920. This led to more immigration from Europe. More than 2 million people entered the United States.

FAST FACT
THE LARGEST GROUP OF IMMIGRANTS, ABOUT 5 MILLION, CAME FROM GERMANY. MANY SETTLED IN THE MIDWEST. SOME BOUGHT FARMS. OTHERS LIVED IN CITIES SUCH AS MILWAUKEE, SAINT LOUIS, AND CINCINNATI.

Chinese immigrants helped build the first railroads.

FIGHTING FOR RIGHTS

The United States opened its first national immigration station in January 1892. This was Ellis Island in New York Harbor. The first person to enter the country through Ellis Island was Annie Moore. She was a teenager from County Cork, Ireland.

Each new group of immigrants suffered **discrimination**. Many people mistreated any group who was different. As more immigrants arrived, citizens objected. Laws were passed to limit the number of immigrants who were allowed into the country.

Young immigrants arrive at Ellis Island.

DISCRIMINATION BY QUOTAS

The American government started to limit immigration in the 1800s. They put **quotas** on the number of people in certain groups who could enter the country.

Asians were the first group to suffer this discrimination. The Chinese Exclusion Act of 1882 prevented Chinese immigrants from entering the country. White workers blamed them for low wages.

The Asiatic Barred Zone Act of 1917 barred most Asians from entering the United States. The 1924 Immigration Act barred almost all Asians. The only group not included were people from the Philippines.

FAST FACT

UNDER THE 1924 IMMIGRATION ACT, 70 PERCENT OF IMMIGRANTS WERE FROM GREAT BRITAIN, IRELAND, AND GERMANY.

Japanese immigrants attempt to fight the Immigration Act of 1924.

Mabel Ping-Hua Lee, Activist

Mabel Lee and her family came to New York from China. She worked her entire life for women's suffrage, or the right to vote. But because of the Chinese Exclusion Act, she never became a citizen. She was never able to vote.

TWENTIETH-CENTURY IMMIGRATION LAWS

More immigration happened during and after World War II. Mexican farmworkers were welcomed while American men were at war. Later, during the Cold War, immigrants came from eastern Europe and other countries.

In 1965, the Immigration and Nationality Act banned the quota system. The act helped those with family in the United States and those with certain skills enter the country.

Many people entered the United States unlawfully when immigration laws were strict. In 1986, President Ronald Reagan signed a law. It **pardoned** 3 million undocumented people.

USING DISCRETION

Officials may deport, or remove, undocumented people from the country. They may use **discretion** in deciding whom to remove.

Ronald Reagan signed the Immigration Reform and Control Act. It pardoned many undocumented people. It also increased border security and fines for companies hiring undocumented immigrants.

FAST FACT
BY ABOUT 1985, MORE THAN 80 PERCENT OF DOCTORS IN SOME NEW YORK HOSPITALS WERE ASIAN IMMIGRANTS.

IMMIGRATION SINCE 1996

Two laws in 1996 made immigration policing harsher. Even lawful permanent residents of the United States could be deported, or removed from the country, for minor crimes.

The Development, Relief, and Education for Alien Minors (DREAM) Act was introduced by Representative Luis Gutiérrez in the House of Representatives in 2001. It was meant to help children of undocumented immigrants become citizens. These children are called Dreamers. The act has never passed the Senate.

In 2012, the Obama administration created Deferred Action for Childhood Arrivals (DACA). DACA delays, or slows down, the possibility that children of immigrants could be deported. They can work in the country. They do not have citizenship.

Dreamers visit their deported parents at the U.S.-Mexico border.

RECENT IMMIGRATION NUMBERS

In 2019, the United States had about 44.4 million immigrants. This is one-fifth of all the world's immigrants. It's more than any other country. About three-fourths of U.S. immigrants are here lawfully. The largest populations of immigrants live in cities such as New York, Los Angeles, and Miami.

FOREIGN-BORN POPULATION (2017)

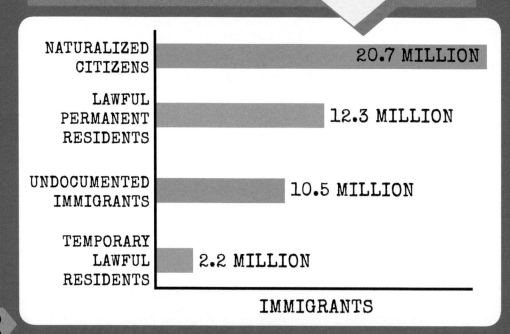

NATURALIZED CITIZENS — 20.7 MILLION

LAWFUL PERMANENT RESIDENTS — 12.3 MILLION

UNDOCUMENTED IMMIGRANTS — 10.5 MILLION

TEMPORARY LAWFUL RESIDENTS — 2.2 MILLION

IMMIGRANTS

WHERE IMMIGRANTS COME FROM (2017)

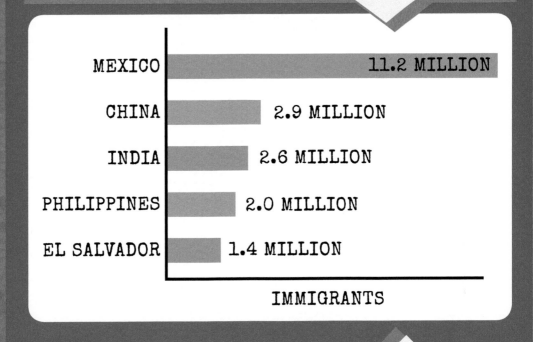

MEXICO	11.2 MILLION
CHINA	2.9 MILLION
INDIA	2.6 MILLION
PHILIPPINES	2.0 MILLION
EL SALVADOR	1.4 MILLION

IMMIGRANTS

Estimates show that the population of the United States is made up of 13.6 percent immigrants.

WHY SO MANY IMMIGRANTS?

Immigrants have always seen the United States as a land of opportunity. They seek better lives, better jobs, more freedom, and more safety. Certain freedoms and rights are written into the U.S. Constitution. These freedoms and rights aren't protected everywhere.

ELLIS ISLAND THEN AND NOW

Most Ellis Island immigrants in 1907 were from Europe. This included Italy, Austria, and Germany. The largest number came from Russia. Only about half spoke English, compared to 84 percent in 2017. Today many immigrants are **professionals**. In 1907, most were laborers.

On the West Coast, immigrants entered the United States through Angel Island between 1910 and 1940.

Lisa Sasaki

Lisa Sasaki is the director of the Smithsonian Asian Pacific American Center. Her great-grandparents were mistreated during World War II. This is because they came from Japan. They gave up their Japanese **traditions** to be accepted as Americans. Sasaki thinks everyone has a right to their own history and **culture**.

 VERIFIED

Smithsonian Asian Pacific American Center:
https://smithsonianapa.org/

STUDENTS AS IMMIGRANTS

The number of U.S. immigrant students is rising. In 1980, 7 percent of schoolchildren were immigrants. In 1990, the number was 11 percent. In 2015, the number rose to 23 percent.

STUDENT IMMIGRANT MOVEMENT

Student Immigrant Movement (SIM) is a group from Massachusetts. Members fight for freedom for undocumented youth ages 13 to 30. They provide youth with protection, leadership training, and **political** education.

HELPING IMMIGRANT STUDENTS

Schools often set up special **programs** to help immigrant students. A Utah school district has a course to introduce immigrant kids to new skills. These include using a locker and riding a school bus. A south Texas district teaches in both Spanish and English. This helps students succeed. Some schools have programs for immigrant parents as well.

A special course helps immigrant boys adjust to high school.

Young immigrant students often live in **poverty**. They have different backgrounds and education levels. Their cultures and religions may be different from most native-born Americans. Many speak little or no English. School is where they learn to be Americans.

REFUGEES TODAY

The number of displaced people in the world is at an all-time high. At the end of 2018, 70.8 million people had left their homes. Almost 30 million of them became refugees. Many refugees are escaping wars. Some face danger from governments or people at home.

Until recently, the United States took in more refugees than all other countries combined. This changed in 2017. The Trump administration allows far fewer refugees to enter the country. It's harder to get accepted. Wait times are longer.

FINDING SAFETY

The United States created the Refugee Resettlement Program in 1980. About 3 million refugees have been resettled. In 2018, 22,491 refugees arrived. More than half came from the Democratic Republic of Congo or Myanmar (Burma).

The number of refugees is growing. More than half of the world's refugees are children under 18.

DEPORTING THE UNDOCUMENTED

Undocumented people are in the country unlawfully. They may be deported.

The number of people deported has gone down. Under President Bill Clinton, 12 million people were deported. Under President George W. Bush, 10 million were deported. Under President Barack Obama, 5 million were deported.

President Obama deported mainly criminals and recent arrivals. President Donald Trump promised to deport as many people as possible.

 VERIFIED

To learn more about U.S. Immigration and Customs Enforcement, visit the official website:
https://www.ice.gov/

U.S. IMMIGRATION & CUSTOM

Immigration and Customs Enforcement (ICE) deports undocumented people. This man is an undocumented immigrant from Mexico. In this image, he's being processed at an ICE center in Pheonix, Arizona.

IMMIGRATION UNDER TRUMP

President Trump is unfriendly to immigrants. When he became president in 2017, he changed the U.S. immigration policy that had existed for many years.

"AMERICA FIRST"

Trump's "America First" policy is meant to protect American workers by keeping out immigrants. Trump's immigration policy has six major parts:

1. Completing a 2,000-mile (3,200 km) border wall with Mexico.

2. Deporting immigrants who had arrived as children, who are currently protected by DACA.

3. Ordering a travel ban to limit entry of people from other countries, particularly people from Muslim countries.

4. Increasing screening, or checking, of immigrants.

5. Allowing entry to only highly skilled workers.

6. Making it harder to enter the country as a lawful immigrant or refugee.

Congress objected to many of President Trump's **proposals**. Courts overturned, or turned down, parts of the travel ban. They kept DACA. Congress has also argued over the funding of the border wall.

Thousands have protested Trump policies.

FREE OUR FUTURE

ABOLISH ICE

BUILDING A BORDER WALL

President Trump promised to build a wall along the U.S.-Mexico border to stop illegal immigration. By the end of 2020, Trump promised to complete 450 miles (724 km). Only 98 miles (158 km) were complete as of 2019. Some people say the wall won't work. Some also believe it will present problems for the **environment** and animals.

As of early 2020, more than $11 billion had been set aside to build 576 miles (927 km) of wall. This is almost $20 million per mile. If completed, it would be the most expensive wall in the world.

THE WALL AND THE ENVIRONMENT

Many laws to keep the environment safe are no longer being followed along the border. These include laws protecting wildlife and landscapes. Fossils and Native American sacred sites are also unprotected. Air and water pollution are also problems.

The border wall is incomplete and is made of different materials along its length.

CHILDREN IN CAGES

In June 2019, up to 2,000 children per day were being held in U.S. Border Patrol stations. Many of these are in Texas. Kids as young as two or three are parted from their parents or other adults.

The children are kept in jail-like conditions. They sleep on foil blankets, often on floors. They have no private bathrooms. They can't brush their teeth, take baths, or get clean clothes.

POOR HEALTH CARE

Mariee Juárez died at age 19 months. She died from a treatable lung infection. This happened while she was held in a U.S. immigration jail with her mother, Yazmin. They were from Guatemala. Yazmin says she begged medical staff at the jail to treat Mariee, but they did not.

Older children care for younger ones in border camps

IMMIGRANTS HELP AMERICA

Immigrants help the United States in many ways. They live and work here. They raise children and support their communities. They pay taxes.

Immigrants are very important to the country's economy. One of the most common arguments against immigrants is that they take American jobs. However, studies have shown this isn't true. Immigrants usually settle in growing areas. Their presence helps the economy grow.

FACTS ABOUT U.S. IMMIGRANTS

1. They pay more in taxes than they take in government benefits.

2. They make up for a national falling birthrate and shrinking workforce.

3. Immigrant workers take jobs that native citizens don't want.

4. Children born as citizens in the United States to immigrant parents are oten healthier as adults than immigrant children.

Many immigrants begin working in low-paying jobs.

JOBS HELD BY IMMIGRANTS

First-generation immigrants who lack college degrees begin with low-paying jobs, such as:

- Farming and fishing
- Building and grounds care
- Manufacturing clothing or food
- Hotel industry
- Construction

FAMOUS IMMIGRANTS

Levi Strauss was from Germany. He founded the first company to sell blue jeans—Levi's Jeans. Liz Claiborne was from Belgium. She changed women's fashion. She was also the first woman to make the Fortune 500 list.

Sergey Brin is from Russia. He cofounded Google. Jan Koum was born in the Soviet Union, in what is now Ukraine. He cofounded Whatsapp. Steve Chen from Taiwan and Jawed Karim from Germany cofounded YouTube.

Google cofounder Sergey Brin was born in Moscow, Russia. He and his family immigrated to the United States in 1979 to escape anti-Semitism, or prejudice against Jews.

IMMIGRATION AROUND THE WORLD

In the 2010s, immigrants poured into Europe—or tried to. They came from Africa, the Middle East, and South Asia. Many were refugees. Many drowned trying to cross the Mediterranean Sea in small boats.

When they reach Europe, refugees are often not welcome. They are kept in holding centers until a country will accept them. Some countries have laws that limit or ban immigrants from entering. Great Britain accepts very few refugees. Spain, Germany, Italy, and France accept more. In 2018, the United Nations Refugee Agency asked that 32,400 refugees be settled in 30 European countries.

FAST FACT

ALMOST 5.2 MILLION REFUGEES AND MIGRANTS HAD REACHED EUROPE BY THE END OF 2016. IN 2018, MORE THAN 138,000 MIGRANTS TRIED TO TRAVEL BY SEA. MORE THAN 2,000 DROWNED.

African refugees wait for rescue after crossing the Mediterranean.

WHERE DOES AMERICA FIT?

Everyone in the United States (except perhaps Native Americans) has roots elsewhere. Some people are immigrants or children of immigrants. Some are descended from enslaved people. Immigrants have entered America for many reasons, including religious freedom and the search for a better life.

Over the years, some refugee and immigrant groups have been accepted and others have not. But refugees and immigrants value America's freedom and ideals. They work hard and bring new skills and customs to our country. As of 2020, U.S. immigration has slowed. But people are still arguing about it. They ask: How many immigrants should we accept? Where should they come from? What should we do about undocumented immigrants?

Where do you think the United States should stand on the issue of immigration?

The poem on the Statue of Liberty welcomes immigrants with the words "Give me your tired, your poor, Your huddled masses yearning to breathe free, The wretched refuse of your teeming shore. Send these, the homeless, tempest-tost to me, I lift my lamp beside the golden door!"

GLOSSARY

colonial: Relating to an area controlled by another country that's usually far from it.

culture: The beliefs and ways of life of a certain group of people.

custom: An action or way of behaving that's traditional among the people in a certain group or place.

discretion: The right to choose what should be done in a particular situation.

discrimination: Unfair treatment based on factors such as a person's race, age, religion, or gender.

environment: The natural world around us.

famine: A shortage of food that causes people to go hungry.

naturalize: To make a person a citizen.

pardon: To officially say that someone who was charged with a crime will be allowed to go free and will not be punished.

permission: The approval of a person in charge.

political: Of or relating to politics or government.

poverty: The state of being poor.

professional: A person who does a certain job for a living.

program: A plan of action such as a class or course.

proposal: The act of putting something forward for consideration.

protect: To keep safe.

quota: An official limit on the number of amount of people or things that are allowed.

relative: A member of one's family.

religious: Having to do with religion, or an organized system of belief.

tradition: Having to do with the ways of doing things in a culture that are passed down from parents to children.

INDEX